Toasty Toes
SOCKS FOR ALL SEASONS
by Knit Picks

Photography by Amy Cave

Printed in the United States of America

Second Printing, 2016

ISBN 978-1-62767-119-4

Versa Press, Inc

800-447-7829

www.versapress.com

CONTENTS

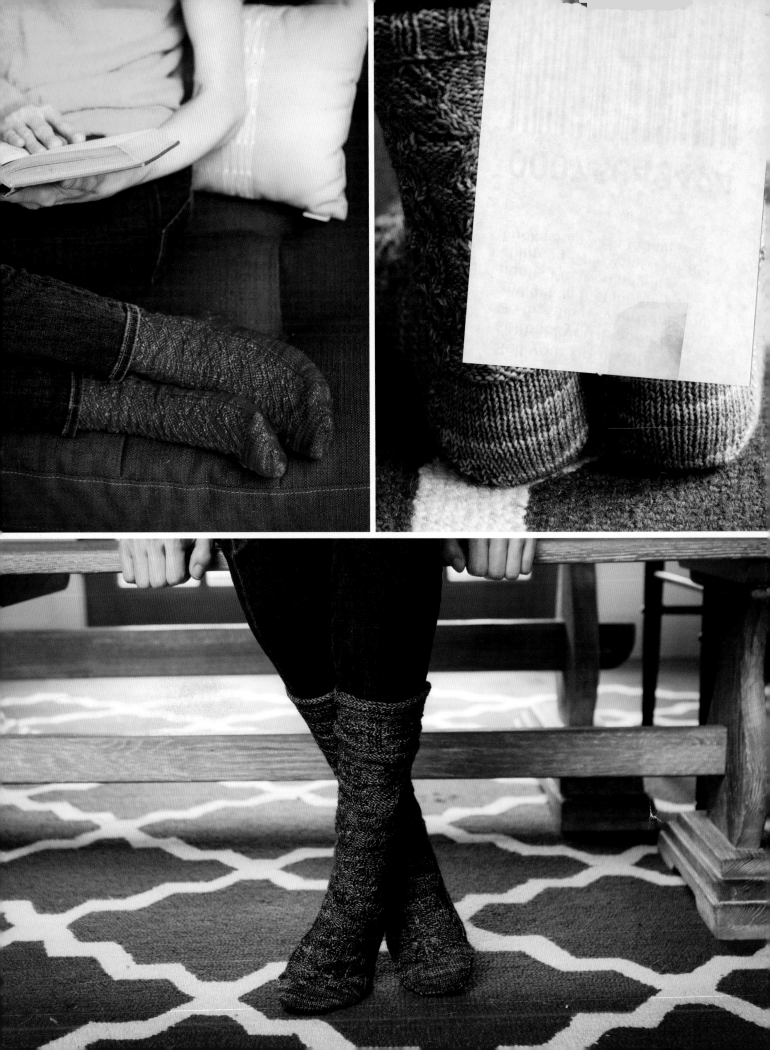

JANUARY: THERMAL SOCKS

by Knit Picks Design Team

FINISHED SIZE

Women's Medium (9.75" long, US size 8.5)

YARN

Knit Picks Hawthorne Multi Fingering (80% Superwash Fine Highland Wool, 20% Polyamide Nylon; 357 yds/100g): Vancouver 26428; 1 skein

NEEDLES

US 2 (2.75 mm): Circular or DPNs

NOTIONS

Yarn Needle
Stitch Markers
Cable Needle

GAUGE

32 sts/40 rows = 4 inches in St st on US 2 unblocked. Check your gauge before you begin.

January: Thermal Socks

Notes

With the insulating powers of the waffle stitch and a delicate cable for decoration, these hearty socks will get you through any long, cold winter.

M1L (Make 1 Left-leaning stitch): PU the bar between st just worked and next st and place on needle as a regular stitch; knit through the back loop.

M1R (Make 1 Right-leaning stitch): PU the bar between st just worked and next st and place on needle backwards (incorrect stitch mount). Knit through the front loop.

DIRECTIONS

Toe

Using Backwards loop CO, cast on 8 sts (for a narrow toe, 10 for average, and 12 for a wider toe). Knit across these sts. Turning work so that cast-on edge is on top and working yarn is to the right of the work, PU and knit into each cast-on st (including the slip knot). You are now working in the round. If using DPNs, arrange so that first 8 (10, 12) sts are distributed over two needles; these will be the instep. You may distribute sole sts over two needles as well if you wish. For two circular needles or magic loop, the first 8 (10, 12) sts are the instep, the second are the sole.

First round: K1, M1L, K to last st of instep, M1R, K1. Repeat for sole sts. Repeat this increase round every round twice more, then every other round until you have reached 60 sts around.

After toe is completed, begin working from Thermal Chart across instep, leaving sole in St st. Work repeats of rounds 1-4 until heel, keeping track of where you are in the pattern.

Heel

When you have worked the sock to about 2" from the back of your heel, you are ready to begin the heel. You do not need to finish a pattern repeat to complete the heel; keep track of where you are in your pattern wherever you stop. The heel is always worked over an even number of sts.

Work across the instep; K to last sole st. Turn work without working that st. On WS, work a backwards YO around the RH needle (yarn in front of the needle, up and over, then pulled behind again to purl) and purl to the last st. Use your finger to stabilize the YO as you work the first purl.

Turn work and work a backwards YO around RH needle (yarn behind the needle, then up and over in front of the needle, then to back to knit) and knit across front to the first stitch-yarn over pair. Turn, work a backwards YO, Purl to first stitch-yarn over pair, turn, and work a backwards YO. Continue in this manner, turning before the next stitch-yarn over pair, until there are 8 sts (for narrow heels, 10 sts for average, 12 sts for wide) between yarn overs (this includes the st in the st-yarn over pairs). The RS should be facing you.

Work across RS to the first YO.

If you need to, correct the stitch mount of the YO; knit it together with the next st. Turn work and backwards-YO; purl to first YO. Correct the stitch mount of the YO if needed, and then SSP: slip the YO as if to knit, the next st as if to knit, return them to the LH needle and purl together through the back loop. Turn work, and backwards YO.

Work to the first YO. There will be two YOs; knit these together with the next st, turn, and backwards YO. All remaining RS rows will be completed in this manner.

Purl to first YO. There will be two YOs; slip these and the following st as if to knit, place back on LH needle, and purl all three together through the back loop. Turn work and backwards YO. All remaining WS rows will be completed in this manner.

Rejoin round

After the last 3 sts on either side have been worked together, there will be two flanking YOs. On the RS, work up to the YO and slip it onto the RH needle. PU 1 st between YO and the first instep st; place this and YO on LH needle and knit them tog with the first st of instep. (If pattern states that first st is not a knit, work as stated in the pattern.) Work in pattern across instep to last st. Slip this st to RH needle, PU 1 st in the gap between the st and the YO on the heel needle, and then move the YO to the instep needle. Pass these three sts onto LH needle and knit them together.

After heel is completed, finish the pattern repeat you're on and work one more across instep only.

Begin working repeats of these 30 sts twice around sock; work for about 5" in pattern.

Thermal Ribbing

Multiple of 4 sts.
Round 1: *K2, P1, K1; Rep from *.
Round 2: *K1, P3; Rep from *.

Work in Thermal Ribbing for two inches.

BO loosely in rib.

Finishing

Weave in ends, wash and block.

Thermal Chart

30	29	28	27	26	25	24	23	22	21	20	19	18	17	16	15	14	13	12	11	10	9	8	7	6	5	4	3	2	1	
																														4
																														3
																														2
																														1

Legend

purl
purl stitch

knit
knit stitch

kfb
Knit into the front and back of the stitch

k2tog
Knit two stitches together as one stitch

p2tog tbl
Purl two stitches together in back loops, inserting needle from the left, behind and into the backs of the 2nd & 1st stitches in that order

c2 over 2 right
sl2 to CN, hold in back. k2, k2 from CN

c2 over 2 left
sl 2 to CN, hold in front. k2, k2 from CN

FEBRUARY: HEARTS ABOUND SOCKS

by Knit Picks Design Team

FINISHED SIZE
Women's Medium (9.75" long, US size 8.5)

YARN
Knit Picks Hawthorne Multi Fingering (80% Superwash Fine Highland Wool, 20% Polyamide Nylon; 357 yds/100g): Parkrose 26681; 1 skein

NEEDLES
US 2 (2.75 mm): Circular or DPNs

NOTIONS
Yarn Needle
Stitch Markers
Cable Needle

GAUGE
32 sts/40 rows = 4 inches in St st on US 2 unblocked. Check your gauge before you begin.

February: Hearts Abound Socks

Notes

Lacy hearts grace these wonderful socks from top to toes, finished with a sweet picot bind-off. A simple design with gorgeous results that you will love to wear!

M1L (Make 1 Left-leaning stitch): PU the bar between st just worked and next st and place on needle as a regular stitch; knit through the back loop.

M1R (Make 1 Right-leaning stitch): PU the bar between st just worked and next st and place on needle backwards (incorrect stitch mount). Knit through the front loop.

Toe

Using Backwards loop CO, cast on 8 sts (for a narrow toe, 10 for average, and 12 for a wider toe). Knit across these sts. Turning work so that cast-on edge is on top and working yarn is to the right of the work, PU and knit into each cast-on st (including the slip knot). You are now working in the round. If using DPNs, arrange so that first 8 (10, 12) sts are distributed over two needles; these will be the instep. You may distribute sole sts over two needles as well if you wish. For two circular needles or magic loop, the first 8 (10, 12) sts are the instep, the second are the sole.

First round: K1, M1L, K to last st of instep, M1R, K1. Repeat for sole sts. Repeat this increase round every round twice more, then every other round until you have reached 60 sts around (64 for wider feet). Some patterns require 64 or more stitches to complete; this is noted in individual pattern sections.

After toe is completed, begin working from Hearts Chart across instep, leaving sole in St st. Rearrange sts so that there are 31 sts on the instep side. Work repeats of rounds 1-20 until heel, keeping track of where you are in the pattern. When you get to the heel, rearrange sts ao that heel can be worked over 30 sts.

Heel

When you have worked the sock to about 2" from the back of your heel, you are ready to begin the heel. You do not need to finish a pattern repeat to complete the heel; keep track of where you are in your pattern wherever you stop. The heel is always worked over an even number of sts.

Work across the instep; K to last sole st. Turn work without working that st. On WS, work a backwards YO around the RH needle (yarn in front of the needle, up and over, then pulled behind again to purl) and purl to the last st. Use your finger to stabilize the YO as you work the first purl.

Turn work and work a backwards YO around RH needle (yarn behind the needle, then up and over in front of the needle, then to back to knit) and knit across front to the first stitch-yarn over pair. Turn, work a backwards YO, Purl to first stitch-yarn over pair, turn, and work a backwards YO. Continue in this manner, turning before the next stitch-yarn over pair, until there are 8 sts (for narrow heels, 10 sts for average, 12 sts for wide) between

yarn overs (this includes the st in the st-yarn over pairs). The RS should be facing you.

Work across RS to the first YO.

If you need to, correct the stitch mount of the YO; knit it together with the next st. Turn work and backwards-YO; purl to first YO. Correct the stitch mount of the YO if needed, and then SSP: slip the YO as if to knit, the next st as if to knit, return them to the LH needle and purl together through the back loop. Turn work, and backwards YO.

Work to the first YO. There will be two YOs; knit these together with the next st, turn, and backwards YO. All remaining RS rows will be completed in this manner.

Purl to first YO. There will be two YOs; slip these and the following st as if to knit, place back on LH needle, and purl all three together through the back loop. Turn work and backwards YO. All remaining WS rows will be completed in this manner.

Rejoin round

After the last 3 sts on either side have been worked together, there will be two flanking YOs. On the RS, work up to the YO and slip it onto the RH needle. PU 1 st between YO and the first instep st; place this and YO on LH needle and knit them tog with the first st of instep. (If pattern states that first st is not a knit, work as stated in the pattern.) Work in pattern across instep to last st. Slip this st to RH needle, PU 1 st in the gap between the st and the YO on the heel needle, and then move the YO to the instep needle. Pass these three sts onto LH needle and knit them together.

After heel is completed, rearrange sts so there are 31 sts across instep and finish the pattern repeat you're on. Work one more across instep only.

Begin next repeat of pattern, working sts 1-31 across instep and sts 2-30 again across heel side. Work three pattern repeats.

Purl three rounds and knit one, then begin working from Heart Border Chart; repeat these 20 sts three times around sock. Purl three rounds.

Picot Bind Off

Work around sock as follows:
BO 2 st, * Pass st back to LH needle, CO 2 sts, BO4; rep from * around.

Finishing

Weave in ends, wash and block.

Legend

k2tog
Knit two stitches together as one stitch

Central Double Dec
Slip first and second stitches together as if to knit. Knit 1 stitch. Pass two slipped stitches over the knit stitch.

p2tog tbl
Purl two stitches together in back loops, inserting needle from the left, behind and into the backs of the 2nd & 1st stitches in that order

ssk
Slip one stitch as if to knit, Slip another stitch as if to knit. Insert left-hand needle into front of these 2 stitches and knit them together

purl
purl stitch

knit
knit stitch

YO
yarn over

Heart Border Chart

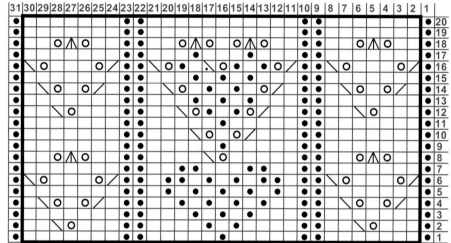

Hearts Chart   Thick outline denotes heel side sts.

MARCH: EVERGREEN SOCKS

by Knit Picks Design Team

FINISHED SIZE
Women's Medium (9.75" long, US size 8.5)

YARN
Knit Picks Hawthorne Multi Fingering
(80% Superwash Fine Highland Wool, 20%
Polyamide Nylon; 357 yds/100g): Mt. Tabor
26444; 1 skein

NEEDLES
US 2 (2.75 mm): Circular or DPNs

NOTIONS
Yarn Needle
Stitch Markers
Cable Needle

GAUGE
32 sts/40 rows = 4 inches in St st on US 2
unblocked. Check your gauge before you
begin.

March: Evergreen Socks

Notes

These beautiful socks use a simple lace pattern to replicate the majestic canopy of a forest with a delicate picot edge to finish them off.

M1L (Make 1 Left-leaning stitch): PU the bar between st just worked and next st and place on needle as a regular stitch; knit through the back loop.

M1R (Make 1 Right-leaning stitch): PU the bar between st just worked and next st and place on needle backwards (incorrect stitch mount). Knit through the front loop.

DIRECTIONS

Toe

Using Backwards loop CO, cast on 8 sts (for a narrow toe, 10 for average, and 12 for a wider toe). Knit across these sts. Turning work so that cast-on edge is on top and working yarn is to the right of the work, PU and knit into each cast-on st (including the slip knot). You are now working in the round. If using DPNs, arrange so that first 8 (10, 12) sts are distributed over two needles; these will be the instep. You may distribute sole sts over two needles as well if you wish. For two circular needles or magic loop, the first 8 (10, 12) sts are the instep, the second are the sole.

First round: K1, M1L, K to last st of instep, M1R, K1. Repeat for sole sts. Repeat this increase round every round twice more, then every other round until you have reached 60 sts around.

After toe is completed, begin working from Evergreen Chart, working sts 2-30 across instep and leaving sole in St st. You may rearrange sts so that there are 29 sts on the instep side, or work the first st in St st and continue with the chart. Work repeats of rounds 1-20 until heel, keeping track of where you are in the pattern.

Heel

When you have worked the sock to about 2" from the back of your heel, you are ready to begin the heel. You do not need to finish a pattern repeat to complete the heel; keep track of where you are in your pattern wherever you stop. The heel is always worked over an even number of sts.

Work across the instep; K to last sole st. Turn work without working that st. On WS, work a backwards YO around the RH needle (yarn in front of the needle, up and over, then pulled behind again to purl) and purl to the last st. Use your finger to stabilize the YO as you work the first purl.

Turn work and work a backwards YO around RH needle (yarn behind the needle, then up and over in front of the needle, then to back to knit) and knit across front to the first stitch-yarn over pair. Turn, work a backwards YO, Purl to first stitch-yarn over pair, turn, and work a backwards YO. Continue in this manner, turning before the next stitch-yarn over pair, until there are 8 sts (for narrow heels, 10 sts for average, 12 for wide) between yarn overs (this includes the st in the st-yarn over pairs). The RS should be facing you.

Work across RS to the first YO.

If you need to, correct the stitch mount of the YO; knit it together with the next st. Turn work and backwards-YO; purl to first YO. Correct the stitch mount of the YO if needed, and then SSP: slip the YO as if to knit, the next st as if to knit, return them to the LH needle and purl together through the back loop. Turn work, and backwards YO.

Work to the first YO. There will be two YOs; knit these together with the next st, turn, and backwards YO. All remaining RS rows will be completed in this manner.

Purl to first YO. There will be two YOs; slip these and the following st as if to knit, place back on LH needle, and purl all three together through the back loop. Turn work and backwards YO. All remaining WS rows will be completed in this manner.

Rejoin round

After the last 3 sts on either side have been worked together, there will be two flanking YOs. On the RS, work up to the YO and slip it onto the RH needle. PU 1 st between YO and the first instep

Legend

▪	**purl**	purl stitch
■	**No Stitch**	Placeholder - No stitch made.
□	**knit**	knit stitch
◩	**ssk**	Slip one stitch as if to knit, Slip another stitch as if to knit. Insert left-hand needle into front of these 2 stitches and knit them together
◪	**k2tog**	Knit two stitches together as one stitch
◪	**k3tog**	Knit three stitches together as one

⊙	**YO**	yarn over
MR	**make one right**	
ML	**make one left**	
⋀	**Central Double Dec**	Slip first and second stitches together as if to knit. Knit 1 stitch. Pass two slipped stitches over the knit stitch.
—	**pattern repeat**	
◪	**k3tog**	Knit three stitches together as one

st; place this and YO on LH needle and knit them tog with the first st of instep. (If pattern states that first st is not a knit, work as stated in the pattern.) Work in pattern across instep to last st. Slip this st to RH needle, PU 1 st in the gap between the st and the YO on the heel needle, and then move the YO to the instep needle. Pass these three sts onto LH needle and knit them together.

Begin working in the round as usual, following pattern.

After heel is completed, finish the pattern repeat you're on. Work one more across instep only.

Move on to round 21 of Evergreen Chart; work one repeat of rounds 21-34 across instep.

Starting at round 35, the pattern is 30 sts across and will repeat twice around the sock; work to row 69.

Picot Hem

Work 5 rounds in St st.

Next round: *K2tog, YO; repeat from * around. Work four rounds in St st; BO loosely. Fold the fabric along the eyelet row so that BO edge is on the inside of the sock; using yarn tail and yarn needle, stitch BO edge to WS sts so that stitching is invisible on the RS.

Finishing

Weave in ends, wash and block.

Evergreen Chart

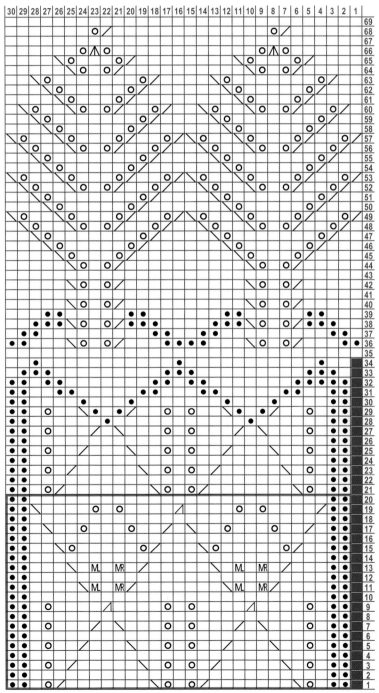

APRIL: BUTTERFLY GARDEN SOCKS

by Knit Picks Design Team

FINISHED SIZE

Women's Medium (9.75" long, US size 8.5)

YARN

Knit Picks Hawthorne Multi Fingering
(80% Superwash Fine Highland Wool, 20%
Polyamide Nylon; 357 yds/100g): Alberta
Arts 26446; 1 skein

NEEDLES:

US 2 (2.75 mm): Circular or DPNs

NOTIONS

Yarn Needle
Stitch Markers
Cable Needle

GAUGE

32 sts/40 rows = 4 inches in St st on US 2
unblocked. Check your gauge before you
begin.

April: Butterfly Garden Socks

Notes

A delicate lace strip reaches from the top of the toes, up the foot to the ankle, meeting up with the beautiful wing span of a butterfly!

For DPN users: This pattern involves cables that cross the center of the instep; this will be across the break between needles. Rearrange your sts as necessary to complete these sts.

M1L (Make 1 Left-leaning stitch): PU the bar between st just worked and next st and place on needle as a regular stitch; knit through the back loop.

M1R (Make 1 Right-leaning stitch): PU the bar between st just worked and next st and place on needle backwards (incorrect stitch mount). Knit through the front loop.

DIRECTIONS

Toe

Using Backwards loop CO, cast on 8 sts (for a narrow toe, 10 for average, and 12 for a wider toe). Knit across these sts. Turning work so that cast-on edge is on top and working yarn is to the right of the work, PU and knit into each cast-on st (including the slip knot). You are now working in the round. If using DPNs, arrange so that first 8 (10, 12) sts are distributed over two needles; these will be the instep. You may distribute sole sts over two needles as well if you wish. For two circular needles or magic loop, the first 8 (10, 12) sts are the instep, the second are the sole.

First round: K1, M1L, K to last st of instep, M1R, K1. Repeat for sole sts. Repeat this increase round every round twice more, then every other round until you have reached 60 sts around.

When toe is completed, knit 10 sts across instep, PM, and begin working from Instep Chart. Repeat this chart up the foot. The sole/heel side sts are knit in St st.

Heel

When you have worked the sock to about 2" from the back of your heel, you are ready to begin the heel. You do not need to finish a pattern repeat to complete the heel; keep track of where you are in your pattern wherever you stop. The heel is always worked over an even number of sts.

Work across the instep; K to last sole st. Turn work without working that st. On WS, work a backwards YO around the RH needle (yarn in front of the needle, up and over, then pulled behind again to purl) and purl to the last st. Use your finger to stabilize the YO as you work the first purl.

Turn work and work a backwards YO around RH needle (yarn behind the needle, then up and over in front of the needle, then to back to knit) and knit across front to the first stitch-yarn over pair. Turn, work a backwards YO, Purl to first stitch-yarn over pair, turn, and work a backwards YO. Continue in this manner, turning before the next stitch-yarn over pair, until there are 8 sts (for narrow heels, 10 sts for average, 12 sts for wide) between yarn overs (this includes the st in the st-yarn over pairs). The RS should be facing you.

Work across RS to the first YO.

If you need to, correct the stitch mount of the YO; knit it together with the next st. Turn work and backwards-YO; purl to first YO. Correct the stitch mount of the YO if needed, and then SSP: slip the YO as if to knit, the next st as if to knit, return them to the LH needle and purl together through the back loop. Turn work, and backwards YO.

Work to the first YO. There will be two YOs; knit these together with the next st, turn, and backwards YO. All remaining RS rows will be completed in this manner.

Purl to first YO. There will be two YOs; slip these and the following st as if to knit, place back on LH needle, and purl all three together through the back loop. Turn work and backwards YO. All remaining WS rows will be completed in this manner.

Rejoin round

After the last 3 sts on either side have been worked together, there will be two flanking YOs. On the RS, work up to the YO and slip it onto the RH needle. PU 1 st between YO and the first instep st; place this and YO on LH needle and knit them tog with the first st of instep. (If pattern states that first st is not a knit, work as stated in the pattern.) Work in pattern across instep to last st. Slip this st to RH needle, PU 1 st in the gap between the st and the YO on the heel needle, and then move the YO to the instep needle. Pass these three sts onto LH needle and knit them together.

Begin working in the round as usual, following pattern. Finish the chart repeat you were working, and work one more.

Next round: begin working from Ankle Chart; repeat twice around foot. Purl one round.

Next round: P2, work across Butterfly Chart, P2; repeat on back of sock. Work to end of chart. Purl three rounds.

Picot Edge

Work 5 rounds in St st.

Next round: *K2tog, YO; repeat from * around. Work four rounds in St st; BO loosely. Fold the fabric along the eyelet row so that BO edge is on the inside of the sock; using yarn tail and yarn needle, stitch BO edge to WS sts so that stitching is invisible on the RS.

Ankle Chart

Instep Chart

Finishing

Weave in ends and block to finished measurements.

Butterfly Chart (worked over 26 sts)

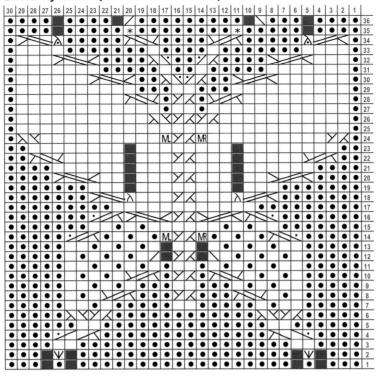

Legend

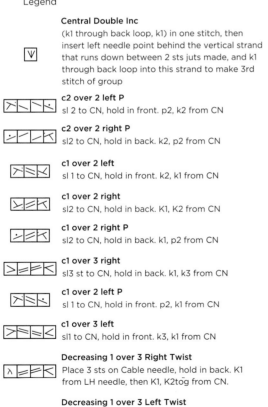

Central Double Inc

Central Double Inc
(k1 through back loop, k1) in one stitch, then insert left needle point behind the vertical strand that runs down between 2 sts juts made, and k1 through back loop into this strand to make 3rd stitch of group

c2 over 2 left P
sl 2 to CN, hold in front. p2, k2 from CN

c2 over 2 right P
sl2 to CN, hold in back. k2, p2 from CN

c1 over 2 left
sl 1 to CN, hold in front. k2, k1 from CN

c1 over 2 right
sl2 to CN, hold in back. K1, K2 from CN

c1 over 2 right P
sl2 to CN, hold in back. k1, p2 from CN

c1 over 3 right
sl3 st to CN, hold in back. k1, k3 from CN

c1 over 2 left P
sl 1 to CN, hold in front. p2, k1 from CN

c1 over 3 left
sl1 to CN, hold in front. k3, k1 from CN

Decreasing 1 over 3 Right Twist
Place 3 sts on Cable needle, hold in back. K1 from LH needle, then K1, K2tog from CN.

Decreasing 1 over 3 Left Twist
Place 1 st on Cable needle, hold in front. K2tog, K1 from LH needle, K1 from CN.

Decreasing 1 over 3 Right Twist, P
Slip three sts to cable needle, hold in back. K 1 st from LH needle, then P1, P2tog from cable needle.

Decreasing 1 over 3 Left Twist, P
Place 1 st on cable needle, hold in front. P1, P2tog from LH needle, K1 from cable needle.

purl
purl stitch

No Stitch
Placeholder - No stitch made.

knit
knit stitch

ssk
Slip one stitch as if to knit, Slip another stitch as if to knit. Insert left-hand needle into front of these 2 stitches and knit them together

k2tog
Knit two stitches together as one stitch

YO
yarn over

MR make one right

ML make one left

Right Twist
Skip the first stitch, knit into 2nd stitch, then knit skipped stitch. Slip both stitches from needle together OR k2tog leaving sts on LH needle, then k first st again, sl both sts off needle.

Left Twist
sl1 to CN, hold in front. k1, k1 from CN

Right Twist, purl bg
sl1 to CN, hold in back. k1, p1 from CN

Left Twist, purl bg
sl1 to CN, hold in front. p1. k1 from CN

Make Knot
Knit 3 sts into one st, turn, P3, turn, Sl2 tog K-wise, K 1, pass 2 slipped sts over.

MAY:
ROSE OF SHARON SOCKS

by Knit Picks Design Team

FINISHED SIZE

Women's Medium (9.75" long, US size 8.5)

YARN

Knit Picks Hawthorne Kettle (80% Superwash Fine Highland Wool, 20% Polyamide Nylon; 357 yds/100g): Turkish Delight 26691; 1 skein

NEEDLES

US 2 (2.75 mm): Circular or DPNs

NOTIONS

Yarn Needle
Stitch Markers
Cable Needle

GAUGE

32 sts/40 rows = 4 inches in St st on US 2 unblocked. Check your gauge before you begin.

May: Rose of Sharon Socks

Notes

The detailed cables of "leaves & vines" wind up the foot, with buds at the ankle and "roses" of bobble clusters that bloom at the top.

For DPN users: this pattern involves cables that cross the center of the instep; this will be across the break between needles. Rearrange your sts as necessary to complete these sts.

M1L (Make 1 Left-leaning stitch): PU the bar between st just worked and next st and place on needle as a regular stitch; knit through the back loop.

M1R (Make 1 Right-leaning stitch): PU the bar between st just worked and next st and place on needle backwards (incorrect stitch mount). Knit through the front loop.

DIRECTIONS

Toe

Using Backwards loop CO, cast on 8 sts (for a narrow toe, 10 for average, and 12 for a wider toe). Knit across these sts. Turning work so that cast-on edge is on top and working yarn is to the right of the work, PU and knit into each cast-on st (including the slip knot). You are now working in the round. If using DPNs, arrange so that first 8 (10, 12) sts are distributed over two needles; these will be the instep. You may distribute sole sts over two needles as well if you wish. For two circular needles or magic loop, the first 8 (10, 12) sts are the instep, the second are the sole.

First round: K1, M1L, K to last st of instep, M1R, K1. Repeat for sole sts. Repeat this increase round every round twice more, then every other round until you have reached 64 sts. After toe, begin working from Leaves chart, keeping in mind that it covers an odd number of stitches. Continue to the heel.

Heel

When you have worked the sock to about 2" from the back of your heel, you are ready to begin the heel. You do not need to finish a pattern repeat to complete the heel; keep track of where you are in your pattern wherever you stop. The heel is always worked over an even number of sts.

Work across the instep; K to last sole st. Turn work without working that st. On WS, work a backwards YO around the RH needle (yarn in front of the needle, up and over, then pulled behind again to purl) and purl to the last st. Use your finger to stabilize the YO as you work the first purl.

Turn work and work a backwards YO around RH needle (yarn behind the needle, then up and over in front of the needle, then to back to knit) and

knit across front to the first stitch-yarn over pair. Turn, work a backwards YO, Purl to first stitch-yarn over pair, turn, and work a backwards YO. Continue in this manner, turning before the next stitch-yarn over pair, until there are 8 sts (for narrow heels, 10 sts for average, 12 for wide) between yarn overs (this includes the st in the st-yarn over pairs). The RS should be facing you.

Work across RS to the first YO.

If you need to, correct the stitch mount of the YO; knit it together with the next st. Turn work and backwards-YO; purl to first YO. Correct the stitch mount of the YO if needed, and then SSP: slip the YO as if to knit, the next st as if to knit, return them to the LH needle and purl together through the back loop. Turn work, and backwards YO.

Work to the first YO. There will be two YOs; knit these together with the next st, turn, and backwards YO. All remaining RS rows will be completed in this manner.

Purl to first YO. There will be two YOs; slip these and the following st as if to knit, place back on LH needle, and purl all three together through the back loop. Turn work and backwards YO. All remaining WS rows will be completed in this manner.

Rejoin round

After the last 3 sts on either side have been worked together, there will be two flanking YOs. On the RS, work up to the YO and slip it onto the RH needle. PU 1 st between YO and the first instep st; place this and YO on LH needle and knit them tog with the first st of instep. (If pattern states that first st is not a knit, work as stated in the pattern.) Work in pattern across instep to last st. Slip this st to RH needle, PU 1 st in the gap between the st and the YO on the heel needle, and then move the YO to the instep needle. Pass these three sts onto LH needle and knit them together.

Leaves Chart

After heel is turned, begin working in the round as usual, following pattern. Finish the repeat of the leaves chart you were working on, and begin working from the buds chart. The first several rows complete the leaves from the previous chart.

At row 16, increase one stitch in the heel portion of the sock - 65 sts.

At row 17, begin working the Bud pattern around the sock; the repeat is outlined. The repeat is from stitches 2-14; consider stitch 1 of the round to be the last st of the fifth repeat of the pattern. You may wish to move the beg of round one stitch to make it easier to remember; move the marker back once these 16 rounds have been completed.

Once the Buds Chart is completed, work from Roses chart; repeat chart five times around sock.

Work one purl round, decreasing one stitch.

Work in K2, P2 rib for one inch; BO loosely in pattern.

Finishing
Weave in ends, wash and block.

Buds Chart

Roses Chart

Legend

Symbol	Name	Description
•	**purl**	purl stitch
▢	**knit**	knit stitch
╲	**ssk**	Slip one stitch as if to knit, slip another stitch as if to knit. Insert left-hand needle into front of these 2 stitches and knit them together
╱	**k2tog**	Knit two stitches together as one stitch
○	**YO**	yarn over
	Right Twist	Skip the first stitch, knit into 2nd stitch, then knit skipped stitch. Slip both stitches from needle together OR k2tog leaving sts on LH needle, then k first st again, sl both sts off needle.
	Left Twist	sl1 to CN, hold in front. k1, k1 from CN
	Right Twist, purl bg	sl1 to CN, hold in back. k1, p1 from CN
	Left Twist, purl bg	sl1 to CN, hold in front. p1. k1 from CN
V	**slip**	Slip stitch as if to purl, holding yarn in back
⋀	**Central Double Dec**	Slip first and second stitches together as if to knit. Knit 1 stitch. Pass two slipped stitches over the knit stitch.
≥	**Make 1 Purlwise**	RS: Perform a lifted bar increase, purling into the new st.
	c1 over 2 right P	RS: sl2 to CN, hold in back. k1, p2 from CN
	c1 over 2 left P	RS: sl 1 to CN, hold in front. p2, k1 from CN
*	**Make Knot**	RS: Knit 3 sts into one st, turn, P3, turn, Sl2 tog K-wise, K 1, pass 2 slipped sts over.
◇	**bobble**	K5 sts into one; turn and P5. Turn and K5, turn and P5 once more, turn. Slip 2 sts k-wise to RH needle, K the next 3 sts tog, pass 2 slipped stitches over.
——	**pattern repeat**	

JUNE: WILDFLOWER SOCKS

by Knit Picks Design Team

FINISHED SIZE

Women's Medium (9.75" long, US size 8.5)

YARN

Knit Picks Hawthorne Multi Fingering (80% Superwash Fine Highland Wool, 20% Polyamide Nylon; 357 yds/100g): Fremont 26684; 1 skein

NEEDLES

US 2 (2.75 mm): Circular or DPNs

NOTIONS

Yarn Needle
Stitch Markers
Cable Needle

GAUGE

32 sts/40 rows = 4 inches in St st on US 2 unblocked. Check your gauge before you begin.

June: Wildflower Socks

Notes

Like wildflowers fluttering in a breeze, the twists and yarn overs of these socks create a master garden for your feet! A classic rolled cuff finishes off this intricate design.

M1L (Make 1 Left-leaning stitch): PU the bar between st just worked and next st and place on needle as a regular stitch; knit through the back loop.

M1R (Make 1 Right-leaning stitch): PU the bar between st just worked and next st and place on needle backwards (incorrect stitch mount). Knit through the front loop.

Toe

Using Backwards loop CO, cast on 8 sts (for a narrow toe, 10 for average, and 12 for a wider toe). Knit across these sts. Turning work so that cast-on edge is on top and working yarn is to the right of the work, PU and knit into each cast-on st (including the slip knot). You are now working in the round. If using DPNs, arrange so that first 8 (10, 12) sts are distributed over two needles; these will be the instep. You may distribute sole sts over two needles as well if you wish. For two circular needles or magic loop, the first 8 (10, 12) sts are the instep, the second are the sole.

First round: K1, M1L, K to last st of instep, M1R, K1. Repeat for sole sts. Repeat this increase round every round twice more, then every other round until you have reached 60 sts around.

When toe is completed, begin working from Wildflower Chart across instep. Repeat the chart until you reach the heel.

The Wildflower chart is worked over 29 sts; you may knit the first instep stitch and then work from the chart, or work the chart and knit the last st, or rearrange the stitches on the needle to accommodate. The heel should be worked over 30 sts; but past the heel, rearrange the stitches so that the 29 stitches are on the instep and 31 stitches are on the heel side.

Heel

When you have worked the sock to about 2" from the back of your heel, you are ready to begin the heel. You do not need to finish a pattern repeat to complete the heel; keep track of where you are in your pattern wherever you stop. The heel is always worked over an even number of sts.

Work across the instep; K to last sole st. Turn work without working that st. On WS, work a backwards YO around the RH needle (yarn in front of the needle, up and over, then pulled behind again to purl) and purl to the last st. Use your finger to stabilize the YO as you work the first purl.

Turn work and work a backwards YO around RH needle (yarn behind the needle, then up and over in front of the needle, then to back to knit) and knit across front to the first stitch-yarn over pair. Turn, work a backwards YO, Purl to first stitch-yarn over pair, turn, and work a backwards YO. Continue in this manner, turning before the next stitch-yarn over pair, until there are 8 sts (for narrow heels, 10 sts for average, 12 sts for wide) between yarn overs (this includes the st in the st-yarn over pairs). The RS should be facing you.

Work across RS to the first YO.

If you need to, correct the stitch mount of the YO; knit it together with the next st. Turn work and backwards-YO; purl to first YO. Correct the stitch mount of the YO if needed, and then SSP: slip the YO as if to knit, the next st as if to knit, return them to the LH needle and purl together through the back loop. Turn work, and backwards YO.

Work to the first YO. There will be two YOs; knit these together with the next st, turn, and backwards YO. All remaining RS rows will be completed in this manner.

Purl to first YO. There will be two YOs; slip these and the following st as if to knit, place back on LH needle, and purl all three together through the back loop. Turn work and backwards YO. All remaining WS rows will be completed in this manner.

Rejoin round

After the last 3 sts on either side have been worked together, there will be two flanking YOs. On the RS, work up to the YO and slip it onto the RH needle. PU 1 st between YO and the first instep st; place this and YO on LH needle and knit them tog with the first st of instep. (If pattern states that first st is not a knit, work as stated in the pattern.) Work in pattern across instep to last st. Slip this st to RH needle, PU 1 st in the gap between the st and the YO on the heel needle, and then move the YO to the instep needle. Pass these three sts onto LH needle and knit them together.

Begin working in the round as usual, following pattern.

When heel is completed, finish the repeat of the Wildflower Chart you are working across the instep. Start the next repeat of the Wildflower chart across instep, and begin working from the Field of Flowers Chart across the heel side. Please note that the two charts do not have the same number of rows.

Work three full repeats of the Wildflower Chart up the ankle (three repeats plus 12 rows of Field of Flowers Chart); 54 rounds.

Rolled Cuff

Purl two rounds; work in St st for 6 rounds and BO loosely.

Finishing

Weave in ends, wash and block.

Field of Flowers Chart

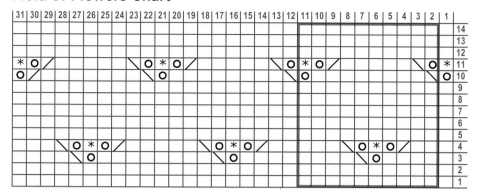

Wildflower Chart

Legend

- **purl** — purl stitch
- **knit** — knit stitch
- **ssk** — Slip one stitch as if to knit, Slip another stitch as if to knit. Insert left-hand needle into front of these 2 stitches and knit them together
- **k2tog** — Knit two stitches together as one stitch
- **YO** — Yarn Over
- **Central Double Dec** — Slip first and second stitches together as if to knit. Knit 1 stitch. Pass two slipped stitches over the knit stitch.
- **Make Knot** — Knit 3 sts into one st, turn, P3, turn, Sl2 tog K-wise, K 1, pass 2 slipped sts over.
- **pattern repeat**

JULY:
STARS AND STRIPES SOCKS

by Knit Picks Design Team

FINISHED SIZE
Women's Medium (9.75" long, US size 8.5)

YARN
Knit Picks Hawthorne Kettle (80% Superwash Fine Highland Wool, 20% Polyamide Nylon; 357 yds/100g): Picnic 26696; 1 skein

NEEDLES
US 2 (2.75 mm): Circular or DPNs

NOTIONS
Yarn Needle
Stitch Markers
Cable Needle

GAUGE
32 sts/40 rows = 4 inches in St st on US 2 unblocked. Check your gauge before you begin.

July: Stars and Stripes Socks

Notes

Oh, say can you see, by the dawn's early light, the proud stars and stripes of these patriotic socks? They're erfect for celebrating the Fourth of July as well as anytime you need a little star-spangled banner in your step. The lacy stars are complemented by waving stripes and finished with a rolled cuff.

M1L (Make 1 Left-leaning stitch): PU the bar between st just worked and next st and place on needle as a regular stitch; knit through the back loop.

M1R (Make 1 Right-leaning stitch): PU the bar between st just worked and next st and place on needle backwards (incorrect stitch mount). Knit through the front loop.

DIRECTIONS

Toe

Using Backwards loop CO, cast on 8 sts (for a narrow toe, 10 for average, and 12 for a wider toe). Knit across these sts. Turning work so that cast-on edge is on top and working yarn is to the right of the work, PU and knit into each cast-on st (including the slip knot). You are now working in the round. If using DPNs, arrange so that first 8 (10, 12) sts are distributed over two needles; these will be the instep. You may distribute sole sts over two needles as well if you wish. For two circular needles or magic loop, the first 8 (10, 12) sts are the instep, the second are the sole.

First round: K1, M1L, K to last st of instep, M1R, K1. Repeat for sole sts. Repeat this increase round every round twice more, then every other round until you have reached 60 sts around (64 for wider feet). Some patterns require 64 or more stitches to complete; this is noted in individual pattern sections.

After toe is completed, begin working from Stars and Stripes Chart across instep sts. The sole/heel side sts are knit in St st. Work until heel, noting what line of the chart you've completed.

Heel

When you have worked the sock to about 2" from the back of your heel, you are ready to begin the heel. You do not need to finish a pattern repeat to complete the heel; keep track of where you are in your pattern wherever you stop. The heel is always worked over an even number of sts.

Work across the instep; K to last sole st. Turn work without working that st. On WS, work a backwards YO around the RH needle (yarn in front of the needle, up and over, then pulled behind again to purl) and purl to the last st. Use your finger to stabilize the YO as you work the first purl.

Turn work and work a backwards YO around RH needle (yarn behind the needle, then up and over in front of the needle, then to back to knit) and knit across front to the first stitch-yarn over pair. Turn, work a backwards YO, Purl to first stitch-yarn over pair, turn, and work a backwards YO. Continue in this manner, turning before the next stitch-yarn over pair, until there are 8 sts

(for narrow heels, 10 sts for average, 12 sts for wide) between yarn overs (this includes the st in the st-yarn over pairs). The RS should be facing you.

Work across RS to the first YO.

If you need to, correct the stitch mount of the YO; knit it together with the next st. Turn work and backwards-YO; purl to first YO. Correct the stitch mount of the YO if needed, and then SSP: slip the YO as if to knit, the next st as if to knit, return them to the LH needle and purl together through the back loop. Turn work, and backwards YO.

Work to the first YO. There will be two YOs; knit these together with the next st, turn, and backwards YO. All remaining RS rows will be completed in this manner.

Purl to first YO. There will be two YOs; slip these and the following st as if to knit, place back on LH needle, and purl all three together through the back loop. Turn work and backwards YO. All remaining WS rows will be completed in this manner.

Rejoin round

After the last 3 sts on either side have been worked together, there will be two flanking YOs. On the RS, work up to the YO and slip it onto the RH needle. PU 1 st between YO and the first instep st; place this and YO on LH needle and knit them tog with the first st of instep. (If pattern states that first st is not a knit, work as stated in the pattern.) Work in pattern across instep to last st. Slip this st to RH needle, PU 1 st in the gap between the st and the YO on the heel needle, and then move the YO to the instep needle. Pass these three sts onto LH needle and knit them together.

Begin working in the round as usual, following pattern.

After the heel is completed, finish the repeat of the Stars and Stripes Chart where you left off across the instep. Work one lengthwise repeat of Stars and Stripes Chart around instep and repeat around heel side of sock.

Begin working from Cuff Chart, repeating the 10 sts 6 times around. Work one lengthwise repeat.

Work 12 rounds in St st and BO loosely for rolled cuff.

Finishing

Weave in ends, wash and block.

Stars and Stripes Chart

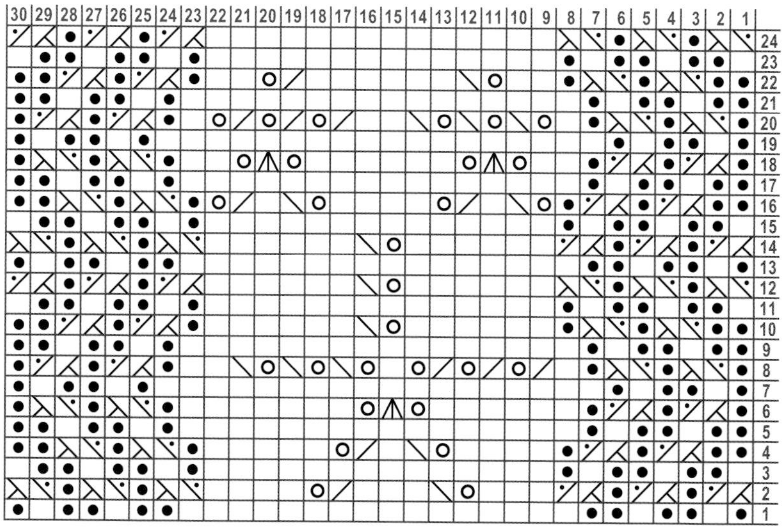

Cuff Chart

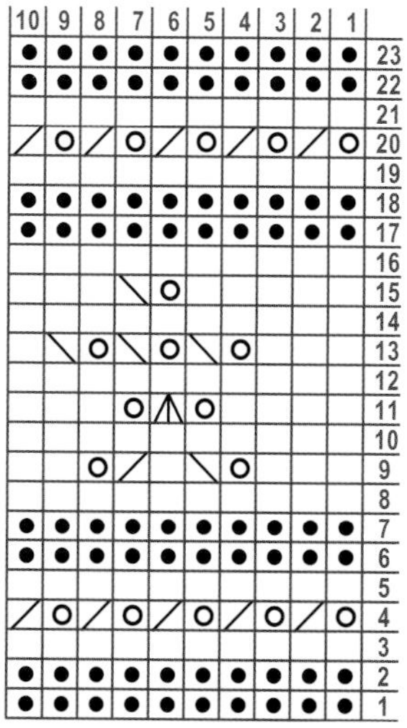

Legend

purl
purl stitch

knit
knit stitch

ssk
Slip one stitch as if to knit, Slip another stitch as if to knit. Insert left-hand needle into front of these 2 stitches and knit them together

k2tog
Knit two stitches together as one stitch

Right Twist, purl bg
sl1 to CN, hold in back. k1, p1 from CN

Left Twist, purl bg
sl1 to CN, hold in front. p1. k1 from CN

Central Double Dec
Slip first and second stitches together as if to knit. Knit 1 stitch. Pass two slipped stitches over the knit stitch.

YO
yarn over

AUGUST: BUSY BEES SOCKS

by Knit Picks Design Team

FINISHED SIZE
Women's Medium (9.75" long, US size 8.5)

YARN
Knit Picks Hawthorne Kettle (80% Superwash Fine Highland Wool, 20% Polyamide Nylon; 357 yds/100g): Compass 26690; 1 skein

NEEDLES
US 2 (2.75 mm): Circular or DPNs

NOTIONS
Yarn Needle
Stitch Markers
Cable Needle

GAUGE
32 sts/40 rows = 4 inches in St st on US 2 unblocked. Check your gauge before you begin.

s Socks

...ul cable from the foot up ... in the honeycomb. They're ...zzing around!

... you may want to go up a ...

... and drop YO's off needle.

... cables that cross the center of the instep, this will be ... eak between needles. Rearrange your sts as necessary to complete these sts.

M1L (Make 1 Left-leaning stitch): PU the bar between st just worked and next st and place on needle as a regular stitch; knit through the back loop.

M1R (Make 1 Right-leaning stitch): PU the bar between st just worked and next st and place on needle backwards (incorrect stitch mount). Knit through the front loop.

DIRECTIONS

Toe
Using Backwards loop CO, cast on 8 sts (for a narrow toe, 10 for average, and 12 for a wider toe). Knit across these sts. Turning work so that cast-on edge is on top and working yarn is to the right of the work, PU and knit into each cast-on st (including the slip knot). You are now working in the round. If using DPNs, arrange so that first 8 (10, 12) sts are distributed over two needles; these will be the instep. You may distribute sole sts over two needles as well if you wish. For two circular needles or magic loop, the first 8 (10, 12) sts are the instep, the second are the sole.

First round: K1, M1L, K to last st of instep, M1R, K1. Repeat for sole sts. Repeat this increase round every round twice more, then every other round until you have reached 60 sts around.

After toe is completed, begin working from Honeycomb Chart across instep sts; work in St st across sole. Work up to the heel, keeping in mind where you left off in the pattern.

Heel
When you have worked the sock to about 2" from the back of your heel, you are ready to begin the heel. You do not need to finish a pattern repeat to complete the heel; keep track of where you are in your pattern wherever you stop. The heel is always worked over an even number of sts.

Work across the instep; K to last sole st. Turn work without working that st. On WS, work a backwards YO around the RH needle (yarn in front of the needle, up and over, then pulled behind again to purl) and purl to the last st. Use your finger to stabilize the YO as you work the first purl.

Turn work and work a backwards YO around RH needle (yarn behind the needle, then up and over in front of the needle, then to back to knit) and knit across front to the first stitch-yarn over pair. Turn, work a backwards YO, Purl to first stitch-yarn over pair, turn, and work a backwards YO. Continue in this manner,

turning before the next stitch-yarn over pair, until there are 8 sts (for narrow heels, 10 sts for average, 12 sts for wide) between yarn overs (this includes the st in the st-yarn over pairs). The RS should be facing you.

Work across RS to the first YO.

If you need to, correct the stitch mount of the YO; knit it together with the next st. Turn work and backwards-YO; purl to first YO. Correct the stitch mount of the YO if needed, and then SSP: slip the YO as if to knit, the next st as if to knit, return them to the LH needle and purl together through the back loop. Turn work, and backwards YO.

Work to the first YO. There will be two YOs; knit these together with the next st, turn, and backwards YO. All remaining RS rows will be completed in this manner.

Purl to first YO. There will be two YOs; slip these and the following st as if to knit, place back on LH needle, and purl all three together through the back loop. Turn work and backwards YO. All remaining WS rows will be completed in this manner.

Rejoin round
After the last 3 sts on either side have been worked together, there will be two flanking YOs. On the RS, work up to the YO and slip it onto the RH needle. PU 1 st between YO and the first instep st; place this and YO on LH needle and knit them tog with the first st of instep. (If pattern states that first st is not a knit, work as stated in the pattern.) Work in pattern across instep to last st. Slip this st to RH needle, PU 1 st in the gap between the st and the YO on the heel needle, and then move the YO to the instep needle. Pass these three sts onto LH needle and knit them together.

Begin working in the round as usual, following pattern.

After the heel, continue with the pattern repeat where you left off across the instep; work one more repeat on the instep side only. Work three more repeats across the instep and across the heel side.

Beehive
After last rep of Honeycomb chart, Knit 2 rounds and Purl 4; rep these 6 rnds two times more. K two rounds.

Begin working from Busy Bees chart, repeating these 15 sts 4 times around sock. Work one vertical repeat.

Work three repeats of the Beehive rounds (K 2 rnds, P 4 rnds), end by purling 6 rnds.

BO loosely.

Finishing
Weave in ends, wash and block.

Busy Bees Chart

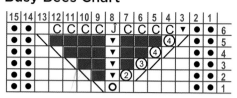

Honeycomb Chart

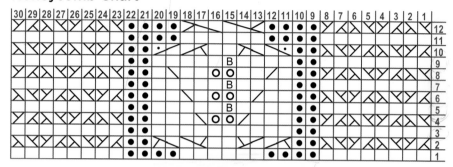

Legend

purl	purl stitch	**knit tbl**	Knit stitch through back loop

purl
purl stitch

knit
knit stitch

ssk
Slip one stitch as if to knit, Slip another stitch as if to knit. Insert left-hand needle into front of these 2 stitches and knit them together

k2tog
Knit two stitches together as one stitch

Right Twist
Skip the first stitch, knit into 2nd stitch, then knit skipped stitch. Slip both stitches from needle together OR k2tog leaving sts on LH needle, then k first st again, sl both sts off needle.

Left Twist
sl1 to CN, hold in front. k1, k1 from CN

c2 over 2 right
sl2 to CN, hold in back. k2, k2 from CN

c2 over 2 left
sl 2 to CN, hold in front. k2, k2 from CN

knit tbl
Knit stitch through back loop

c2 over 2 left P
sl 2 to CN, hold in front. p2, k2 from CN

c2 over 2 right P
sl2 to CN, hold in back. k2, p2 from CN

c3 over 3 left
sl3 to CN, hold in front. k3, k3 from CN

Multiple YO
Yarn Over as many times as indicated in the circle

Drop YO
Drop all YOs from prev row off LH needle without working.

Cable Cast On
Turn work and cast on sts by drawing loop from back to front between two sts.

PU Dropped YOs
Insert RH needle under 5 loose strands of dropped YOs and draw a loop through; place on LH needle.

YO
yarn over

No Stitch
Placeholder - No stitch made.

SEPTEMBER: FIRST HARVEST SOCKS

by Knit Picks Design Team

FINISHED SIZE
Women's Medium (9.75" long, US size 8.5)

YARN
Knit Picks Hawthorne Multi Fingering (80% Superwash Fine Highland Wool, 20% Polyamide Nylon; 357 yds/100g): Rose City 26432; 1 skein

NEEDLES
US 2 (2.75 mm): Circular or DPNs

NOTIONS
Yarn Needle
Stitch Markers
Cable Needle

GAUGE
32 sts/40 rows = 4 inches in St st on US 2 unblocked. Check your gauge before you begin.

September: First Harvest Socks

Notes

Rows of wheat and orchard trees decorate the instep and cuff of these socks with a wonderful texture. Wear these socks while enjoying the first crisp autumn days.

M1L (Make 1 Left-leaning stitch): PU the bar between st just worked and next st and place on needle as a regular stitch; knit through the back loop.

M1R (Make 1 Right-leaning stitch): PU the bar between st just worked and next st and place on needle backwards (incorrect stitch mount). Knit through the front loop.

DIRECTIONS

Toe

Using Backwards loop CO, cast on 8 sts (for a narrow toe, 10 for average, and 12 for a wider toe). Knit across these sts. Turning work so that cast-on edge is on top and working yarn is to the right of the work, PU and knit into each cast-on st (including the slip knot). You are now working in the round. If using DPNs, arrange so that first 8 (10, 12) sts are distributed over two needles; these will be the instep. You may distribute sole sts over two needles as well if you wish. For two circular needles or magic loop, the first 8 (10, 12) sts are the instep, the second are the sole.

First round: K1, M1L, K to last st of instep, M1R, K1. Repeat for sole sts. Repeat this increase round every round twice more, then every other round until you have reached 60 sts around.

Once toe is completed, begin working from Wheat Chart at round 1 across instep sts. Repeat rounds 12-23 until heel, noting what round you're on.

Heel

When you have worked the sock to about 2" from the back of your heel, you are ready to begin the heel. You do not need to finish a pattern repeat to complete the heel; keep track of where you are in your pattern wherever you stop. The heel is always worked over an even number of sts.

Work across the instep; K to last sole st. Turn work without working that st. On WS, work a backwards YO around the RH needle (yarn in front of the needle, up and over, then pulled behind again to purl) and purl to the last st. Use your finger to stabilize the YO as you work the first purl.

Turn work and work a backwards YO around RH needle (yarn behind the needle, then up and over in front of the needle, then to back to knit) and knit across front to the first stitch-yarn over pair. Turn, work a backwards YO, Purl to first stitch-yarn over pair, turn, and work a backwards YO. Continue in this manner, turning before the next stitch-yarn over pair, until there are 8 sts (for narrow heels, 10 sts for average, 12 sts for wide) between yarn overs (this includes the st in the st-yarn over pairs). The RS should be facing you.

Work across RS to the first YO.

If you need to, correct the stitch mount of the YO; knit it together with the next st. Turn work and backwards-YO; purl to first YO. Correct the stitch mount of the YO if needed, and then SSP: slip the YO as if to knit, the next st as if to knit, return them to the LH needle and purl together through the back loop. Turn work, and backwards YO.

Work to the first YO. There will be two YOs; knit these together with the next st, turn, and backwards YO. All remaining RS rows will be completed in this manner.

Purl to first YO. There will be two YOs; slip these and the following st as if to knit, place back on LH needle, and purl all three together through the back loop. Turn work and backwards YO. All remaining WS rows will be completed in this manner.

Rejoin round

After the last 3 sts on either side have been worked together, there will be two flanking YOs. On the RS, work up to the YO and slip it onto the RH needle. PU 1 st between YO and the first instep st; place this and YO on LH needle and knit them tog with the first st of instep. (If pattern states that first st is not a knit, work as stated in the pattern.) Work in pattern across instep to last st. Slip this st to RH needle, PU 1 st in the gap between the st and the YO on the heel needle, and then move the YO to the instep needle. Pass these three sts onto LH needle and knit them together.

Once heel is complete, continue where you left off in the Wheat Chart. Work three more repeats of rounds 12-23 on both the instep and heel side. Once those are completed, work from Wheat chart rounds 24-34.

Work next round as follows: *K1, P11, K6, P11, K1; rep from *.

Begin working from Orchard Chart on both sides of the sock.

Repeat round 26 of Orchard chart for 6 rows. BO loosely in pattern.

Finishing

Weave in ends and block.

Orchard Chart

Wheat Chart

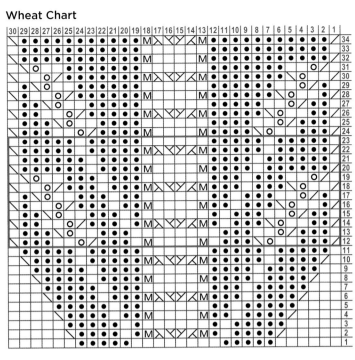

Legend

	c2 over 2 right
	sl2 to CN, hold in back. k2, k2 from CN
	c2 over 2 left
	sl 2 to CN, hold in front. k2, k2 from CN
	c2 over 2 right P
	sl2 to CN, hold in back. k2, p2 from CN
	c2 over 2 left P
	sl 2 to CN, hold in front. p2, k2 from CN
	c1 over 2 right P
	sl2 to CN, hold in back. k1, p2 from CN
	c1 over 2 left P
	sl 1 to CN, hold in front. p2, k1 from CN
	c1 over 2 right
	sl2 to CN, hold in back. k1, k2 from CN
	c1 over 2 left
	sl 1 to CN, hold in front. k2, k1 from CN
•	**purl**
	purl stitch
	knit
	knit stitch
	Right Twist, purl bg
	sl1 to CN, hold in back. k1, p1 from CN
	Left Twist, purl bg
	sl1 to CN, hold in front. p1. k1 from CN

	ssk
\	Slip one stitch as if to knit, Slip another stitch as if to knit. Insert left-hand needle into front of these 2 stitches and knit them together
/	**k2tog**
	Knit two stitches together as one stitch
o	**YO**
	yarn over
	Right Twist
	Skip the first stitch, knit into 2nd stitch, then knit skipped stitch. Slip both stitches from needle together OR k2tog leaving sts on LH needle, then k first st again, sl both sts off needle.
	Left Twist
	sl1 to CN, hold in front. k1, k1 from CN
M	**make one**
	Make one by lifting strand in between stitch just worked and the next stitch, knit into back of this thread.
*	**Make Knot**
	Knit 3 sts into one st, turn, P3, turn, Sl2 tog K-wise, K 1, pass 2 slipped sts over.
—	**pattern repeat**

OCTOBER: FALLING LEAVES SOCKS

by Knit Picks Design Team

FINISHED SIZE

Women's Medium (9.75" long, US size 8.5)

YARN

Knit Picks Hawthorne Multi Fingering
(80% Superwash Fine Highland Wool,
20% Polyamide Nylon; 357 yds/100g):
Laurelhurst 26445; 1 skein

NEEDLES

US 2 (2.75 mm): Circular or DPNs

NOTIONS

Yarn Needle
Stitch Markers
Cable Needle

GAUGE

32 sts/40 rows = 4 inches in St st on US 2
unblocked. Check your gauge before you
begin.

October: Falling Leaves Socks

Notes

The creative twists and turns of the cable pattern on these socks creates a cascade of leaves falling from ankle to toe. The crowning glory is the creative acorn pattern that dances around the cuff for a finishing touch.

M1L (Make 1 Left-leaning stitch): PU the bar between st just worked and next st and place on needle as a regular stitch; knit through the back loop.

M1R (Make 1 Right-leaning stitch): PU the bar between st just worked and next st and place on needle backwards (incorrect stitch mount). Knit through the front loop.

DIRECTIONS

Toe

Using Backwards loop CO, cast on 8 sts (for a narrow toe, 10 for average, and 12 for a wider toe). Knit across these sts. Turning work so that cast-on edge is on top and working yarn is to the right of the work, PU and knit into each cast-on st (including the slip knot). You are now working in the round. If using DPNs, arrange so that first 8 (10, 12) sts are distributed over two needles; these will be the instep. You may distribute sole sts over two needles as well if you wish. For two circular needles or magic loop, the first 8 (10, 12) sts are the instep, the second are the sole.

First round: K1, M1L, K to last st of instep, M1R, K1. Repeat for sole sts. Repeat this increase round every round twice more, then every other round until you have reached 60 sts around.

After toe is completed, begin working from Falling Leaves Chart across instep, leaving sole in St st. Work repeats of rounds 38-59 until heel, keeping track of where you are in the pattern.

Heel

When you have worked the sock to about 2" from the back of your heel, you are ready to begin the heel. You do not need to finish a pattern repeat to complete the heel; keep track of where you are in your pattern wherever you stop. The heel is always worked over an even number of sts.

Work across the instep; K to last sole st. Turn work without working that st. On WS, work a backwards YO around the RH needle (yarn in front of the needle, up and over, then pulled behind again to purl) and purl to the last st. Use your finger to stabilize the YO as you work the first purl.

Turn work and work a backwards YO around RH needle (yarn behind the needle, then up and over in front of the needle, then to back to knit) and knit across front to the first stitch-yarn over pair. Turn, work a backwards YO, Purl to first stitch-yarn over pair, turn, and work a backwards YO. Continue in this manner, turning before the next stitch-yarn over pair, until there are 8 sts (for narrow heels, 10 sts for average, 12 sts for wide) between yarn overs (this includes the st in the st-yarn over pairs). The RS should be facing you.

Work across RS to the first YO.

If you need to, correct the stitch mount of the YO; knit it together with the next st. Turn work and backwards-YO; purl to first YO. Correct the stitch mount of the YO if needed, and then SSP: slip the YO as if to knit, the next st as if to knit, return them to the LH needle and purl together through the back loop. Turn work, and backwards YO.

Work to the first YO. There will be two YOs; knit these together with the next st, turn, and backwards YO. All remaining RS rows will be completed in this manner.

Purl to first YO. There will be two YOs; slip these and the following st as if to knit, place back on LH needle, and purl all three together through the back loop. Turn work and backwards YO. All remaining WS rows will be completed in this manner.

After heel is complete, finish the pattern repeat you're on.

Rejoin round

After the last 3 sts on either side have been worked together, there will be two flanking YOs. On the RS, work up to the YO and slip it onto the RH needle. PU 1 st between YO and the first instep st; place this and YO on LH needle and knit them tog with the first st of instep. (If pattern states that first st is not a knit, work as stated in the pattern.) Work in pattern across instep to last st. Slip this st to RH needle, PU 1 st in the gap between the st and the YO on the heel needle, and then move the YO to the instep needle. Pass these three sts onto LH needle and knit them together.

Begin working in the round as usual, following pattern.

Work repeats of rows 38-59, sts 11-20; repeat these 10 sts 6 times around sock, and work these 22 rounds once.

Move on to round 60 of the chart. Across the 30 instep sts, work from sts 1-30, rows 60-89; across 30 heel side sts, work three repeats of sts 11-20, rows 38-59. This will give you an oak leaf on the front of the sock and smaller leaves around the back. When you have finished one vertical repeat across the heel, continue across the front of the sock as shown and work the heel side in reverse stockinette. Work to end of Falling Leaves Chart.

Eyelet Welt

Work Eyelet Welt over three rounds:
Round 1: Knit.
Round 2: K2tog, YO around.
Round 3: Knit.

Acorn Border

Purl one round.
Begin working from Acorn Chart: repeat these 15 sts 4 times around sock, and these 21 rounds once. Purl one round. Note: row 17, stitch 1, of the chart is half of a twist st - slip the first st and work it together with st 15 of the last pattern repeat.

Work an Eyelet Welt over the next three rounds.

Purl 7 rounds. BO loosely.

Finishing

Weave in ends, wash and block.

Legend

⊡	**purl**	purl stitch
☐	**knit**	knit stitch
⟍	**ssk**	Slip one stitch as if to knit, Slip another stitch as if to knit. Insert left-hand needle into front of these 2 stitches and knit them together
⟋	**k2tog**	Knit two stitches together as one stitch
Ⓜ	**make one right**	
Ⓜ	**make one left**	
⟍⟋	**Right Twist**	Skip the first stitch, knit into 2nd stitch, then knit skipped stitch. Slip both stitches from needle together OR k2tog leaving sts on LH needle, then k first st again, sl both sts off needle.
⟋⟍	**Left Twist**	sl1 to CN, hold in front. k1, k1 from CN
⟋⟍	**Right Twist, purl bg**	sl1 to CN, hold in back. k1, p1 from CN
⟍⟋	**Left Twist, purl bg**	sl1 to CN, hold in front. p1. k1 from CN
V	**slip**	Slip stitch as if to purl, holding yarn in back
⟍ ⟋	**c2 over 1 left P**	sl2 to CN, hold in front. p1, k2 from CN
⟋ ⟍	**c2 over 1 right P**	sl1 to CN, hold in back. k2, p1 from CN
⟍ ⟋	**c4 over 2 left P**	sl4 to CN, hold in front. p2, then k4 from CN
⟋ ⟍	**c4 over 2 right P**	sl2 to CN, hold in back. k4, then p2 from CN
⟍ ⟍	**c3 over 2 left P**	sl3 to CN, hold in front. p2, then k3 from CN
⟋ ⟍	**c3 over 2 right P**	sl2 to CN, hold in back. k3, then p2 from CN
⟍ ⟍	**c2 over 2 left P**	sl 2 to CN, hold in front. p2, k2 from CN
⟋ ⟍	**c2 over 2 right P**	sl2 to CN, hold in back. k2, p2 from CN
⟍ ⟍	**c1 over 2 left P**	sl 1 to CN, hold in front. p2, k1 from CN
⟋ ⟍	**c1 over 2 right P**	sl2 to CN, hold in back. k1, p2 from CN
⟍ ⟍	**c3 over 2 right**	sl2 to CN, hold in back. k3, then k2 from CN
⟍ ⟍	**c3 over 2 left**	sl3 to CN, hold in front. k2, then k3 from CN
⟋ ⟍	**c2 over 1 right**	sl1 to CN, hold in back. k2, k1 from CN
⟍ ⟋	**c2 over 1 left**	sl2 to CN, hold in front. k1, k2 from CN
⟍ ⟍	**c1 over 2 right**	sl2 to CN, hold in back. k1, k2 from CN
⟍ ⟍	**c1 over 2 left**	sl 1 to CN, hold in front. k2, k1 from CN

Acorn Chart

Falling Leaves Chart

NOVEMBER: BARE BARK SOCKS

by Knit Picks Design Team

FINISHED SIZE
Women's Medium (9.75" long, US size 8.5)

YARN
Knit Picks Hawthorne Kettle (80% Superwash Fine Highland Wool, 20% Polyamide Nylon; 357 yds/100g): Faun 26697; 1 skein

NEEDLES
US 2 (2.75 mm): Circular or DPNs

NOTIONS
Yarn Needle
Stitch Markers
Cable Needle

GAUGE
32 sts/40 rows = 4 inches in St st on US 2 unblocked. Check your gauge before you begin.

November: Bare Bark Socks

Notes

These marvelous socks have a geometric cable pattern moving from the toes to the cuff that resembles the stark beauty of bare trees during winter. A ribbed cuff, knit in pattern, crowns the tops of these socks.

For DPN users: some patterns involve cables that cross the center of the instep; this will be across the break between needles. Rearrange your sts as necessary to complete these sts.

M1L (Make 1 Left-leaning stitch): PU the bar between st just worked and next st and place on needle as a regular stitch; knit through the back loop.

M1R (Make 1 Right-leaning stitch): PU the bar between st just worked and next st and place on needle backwards (incorrect stitch mount). Knit through the front loop.

DIRECTIONS

Toe

Using Backwards loop CO, cast on 8 sts (for a narrow toe, 10 for average, and 12 for a wider toe). Knit across these sts. Turning work so that cast-on edge is on top and working yarn is to the right of the work, PU and knit into each cast-on st (including the slip knot). You are now working in the round. If using DPNs, arrange so that first 8 (10, 12) sts are distributed over two needles; these will be the instep. You may distribute sole sts over two needles as well if you wish. For two circular needles or magic loop, the first 8 (10, 12) sts are the instep, the second are the sole.

First round: K1, M1L, K to last st of instep, M1R, K1. Repeat for sole sts. Repeat this increase round every round twice more, then every other round until you have reached 60 sts around (64 for wider feet). Some patterns require 64 or more stitches to complete; this is noted in individual pattern sections.

After toe is completed, begin working from Trees Chart across instep sts only, adjusting sts so that there are 31 sts across. Work the remaining sts (sole) in St st. Work repeats of rounds 21-32 until heel, keeping track of where you are in the pattern.

Heel

When you have worked the sock to about 2" from the back of your heel, you are ready to begin the heel. You do not need to finish a pattern repeat to complete the heel; keep track of where you are in your pattern wherever you stop. The heel should be worked over 30 sts. When you reach the round where you'd like to place your heel, work to st 30 of the chart, then return the 31st st to the sole side and knit across to begin the heel. on first round after heel is

complete, move the st back to the instep and finish the pattern repeat.

Work across the instep; K to last sole st. Turn work without working that st. On WS, work a backwards YO around the RH needle (yarn in front of the needle, up and over, then pulled behind again to purl) and purl to the last st. Use your finger to stabilize the YO as you work the first purl.

Turn work and work a backwards YO around RH needle (yarn behind the needle, then up and over in front of the needle, then to back to knit) and knit across front to the first stitch-yarn over pair. Turn, work a backwards YO, Purl to first stitch-yarn over pair, turn, and work a backwards YO. Continue in this manner, turning before the next stitch-yarn over pair, until there are 8 sts (for narrow heels, 10 sts for average, 12 for wide) between yarn overs (this includes the st in the st-yarn over pairs). The RS should be facing you.

Work across RS to the first YO.

If you need to, correct the stitch mount of the YO; knit it together with the next st. Turn work and backwards-YO; purl to first YO. Correct the stitch mount of the YO if needed, and then SSP: slip the YO as if to knit, the next st as if to knit, return them to the LH needle and purl together through the back loop. Turn work, and backwards YO.

Work to the first YO. There will be two YOs; knit these together with the next st, turn, and backwards YO. All remaining RS rows will be completed in this manner.

Purl to first YO. There will be two YOs; slip these and the following st as if to knit, place back on LH needle, and purl all three together through the back loop. Turn work and backwards YO. All remaining WS rows will be completed in this manner.

Trees Chart

Rejoin Round

After the last 3 sts on either side have been worked together, there will be two flanking YOs. On the RS, work up to the YO and slip it onto the RH needle. PU 1 st between YO and the first instep st; place this and YO on LH needle and knit them tog with the first st of instep. (If pattern states that first st is not a knit, work as stated in the pattern.) Work in pattern across instep to last st.

Slip this st to RH needle, PU 1 st in the gap between the st and the YO on the heel needle, and then move the YO to the instep needle. Pass these three sts onto LH needle and knit them together.

Begin working in the round as usual, following pattern.

Begin working from Treetop Chart, starting on the row you left off on the Trees Chart before the heel. Repeat sts 1-10 six times around sock. Some of the stitches at the very edges of the instep and heel may require re-arranging the sts to complete; move these sts back to their original position once worked. Work rounds 1-12 four times.

Move on to round 13 of the chart; repeat these 20 sts 3 times around sock. Work one repeat of rounds 13-22; repeat row 22 for one inch.

Finishing

BO loosely in rib. Weave in ends, wash and block.

Treetop Chart

|20|19|18|17|16|15|14|13|12|11|10|9|8|7|6|5|4|3|2|1|

(22-row colorwork/cable chart)

Legend

B — knit tbl
Knit stitch through back loop

Make Star St
(Worked over three sts) Knit next three sts together but do not drop from LH needle. K first st and K next two sts tog.

c2 over 1 left
sl2 to CN, hold in front. k1, k2 from CN

c2 over 1 right
sl1 to CN, hold in back. k2, k1 from CN

c2 over 1 left P
sl2 to CN, hold in front. p1, k2 from CN

c2 over 1 right P
sl1 to CN, hold in back. k2, p1 from CN

c1 over 1 left
sl1 to CN, hold in front. k1, k1 from CN

c1 over 1 right
sl1 to CN, hold in back. k1, k1 from CN

c1 over 1 left P
sl1 to CN, hold in front. p1, k1 from CN

c1 over 1 right P
sl1 to CN, hold in back. k1, p1 from CN

— **pattern repeat**

DECEMBER: SNOWFLAKES SOCKS

by Knit Picks Design Team

FINISHED SIZE

Women's Medium (9.75" long, US size 8.5)

YARN

Knit Picks Hawthorne Multi Fingering
(80% Superwash Fine Highland Wool, 20%
Polyamide Nylon; 357 yds/100g): Sellwood
26687; 1 skein

NEEDLES

US 2 (2.75 mm): Circular or DPNs

NOTIONS

Yarn Needle
Stitch Markers
Cable Needle

GAUGE

32 sts/40 rows = 4 inches in St st on US 2
unblocked. Check your gauge before you
begin.

December: Snowflakes Socks

Notes

Warm up to winter with these fanciful socks. Distinctive cabled snowflakes dance all around your feet in this marvelous pattern.

M1L (Make 1 Left-leaning stitch): PU the bar between st just worked and next st and place on needle as a regular stitch; knit through the back loop.

M1R (Make 1 Right-leaning stitch): PU the bar between st just worked and next st and place on needle backwards (incorrect stitch mount). Knit through the front loop.

DIRECTIONS

Toe

Using Backwards loop CO, cast on 8 sts (for a narrow toe, 10 for average, and 12 for a wider toe). Knit across these sts. Turning work so that cast-on edge is on top and working yarn is to the right of the work, PU and knit into each cast-on st (including the slip knot). You are now working in the round. If using DPNs, arrange so that first 8 (10, 12) sts are distributed over two needles; these will be the instep. You may distribute sole sts over two needles as well if you wish. For two circular needles or magic loop, the first 8 (10, 12) sts are the instep, the second are the sole.

First round: K1, M1L, K to last st of instep, M1R, K1. Repeat for sole sts. Repeat this increase round every round twice more, then every other round until you have reached 60 sts around.

After toe is completed, begin working from Snowflakes Chart across instep, leaving sole in St st. Work repeats of rounds 1-32 until heel, keeping track of where you are in the pattern.

Heel

When you have worked the sock to about 2" from the back of your heel, you are ready to begin the heel. You do not need to finish a pattern repeat to complete the heel; keep track of where you are in your pattern wherever you stop. The heel is always worked over an even number of sts.

Work across the instep; K to last sole st. Turn work without working that st. On WS, work a backwards YO around the RH needle (yarn in front of the needle, up and over, then pulled behind again to purl) and purl to the last st. Use your finger to stabilize the YO as you work the first purl.

Turn work and work a backwards YO around RH needle (yarn behind the needle, then up and over in front of the needle, then to back to knit) and knit across front to the first stitch-yarn over pair. Turn, work a backwards YO, Purl to first stitch-yarn over pair, turn, and work a backwards YO. Continue in this manner, turning before the next stitch-yarn over pair, until there are 8 sts (for narrow heels, 10 sts for average, 12 sts for wide) between yarn overs (this includes the st in the st-yarn over pairs). The RS should be facing you.

Work across RS to the first YO.

If you need to, correct the stitch mount of the YO; knit it together with the next st. Turn work and backwards-YO; purl to first YO.

Correct the stitch mount of the YO if needed, and then SSP: slip the YO as if to knit, the next st as if to knit, return them to the LH needle and purl together through the back loop. Turn work, and backwards YO.

Work to the first YO. There will be two YOs; knit these together with the next st, turn, and backwards YO. All remaining RS rows will be completed in this manner.

Purl to first YO. There will be two YOs; slip these and the following st as if to knit, place back on LH needle, and purl all three together through the back loop. Turn work and backwards YO. All remaining WS rows will be completed in this manner.

Legend

purl	purl stitch
No Stitch	Placeholder - No stitch made.
knit	knit stitch
Right Twist	Skip the first stitch, knit into 2nd stitch, then knit skipped stitch. Slip both stitches from needle together OR k2tog leaving sts on LH needle, then k first st again, sl both sts off needle.
Left Twist	sl1 to CN, hold in front. k1, k1 from CN
Right Twist, purl bg	sl1 to CN, hold in back. k1, p1 from CN
Left Twist, purl bg	sl1 to CN, hold in front. p1. k1 from CN
slip	Slip stitch as if to purl, holding yarn in back
c2 over 1 left P	sl2 to CN, hold in front. p1, k2 from CN
c2 over 1 right P	sl1 to CN, hold in back. k2, p1 from CN
c1 over 2 left P	sl 1 to CN, hold in front. p2, k1 from CN
c1 over 2 right P	sl2 to CN, hold in back. k1, p2 from CN
cluster2	Slip 2 stitches with yarn in back, pass yarn to front, slip same two stitches back to left needle, pass yarn to back, k2
pattern repeat	

Rejoin round

After the last 3 sts on either side have been worked together, there will be two flanking YOs. On the RS, work up to the YO and slip it onto the RH needle. PU 1 st between YO and the first instep st; place this and YO on LH needle and knit them tog with the first st of instep. (If pattern states that first st is not a knit, work as stated in the pattern.) Work in pattern across instep to last st. Slip this st to RH needle, PU 1 st in the gap between the st and the YO on the heel needle, and then move the YO to the instep needle. Pass these three sts onto LH needle and knit them together.

After heel is complete, finish the pattern repeat you're on.

Begin working repeats of rows 33-64, sts 2-31; repeat these 30 sts twice around sock, and repeat these 32 rounds twice. Note that the stitch 1 is actually the last st of the previous pattern repeat; it is included in the chart only to show that there are stitches that cross over the beginning and end of the instep and heel.

After last repeat of Snowflakes Chart is complete, work in P2, K2 ribbing around sock for one inch. BO loosely in rib.

Finishing

Weave in ends, wash and block.

Snowflakes Chart

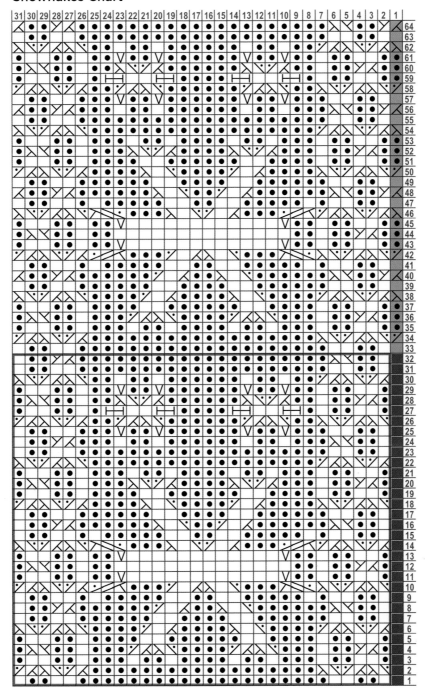

For pattern support, contact customerservice@knitpicks.com

Abbreviations						
BO	bind off	M	marker		stitch	TBL	through back loop
cn	cable needle	M1	make one stitch	RH	right hand	TFL	through front loop
CC	contrast color	M1L	make one left-leaning	rnd(s)	round(s)	tog	together
CDD	Centered double dec		stitch	RS	right side	W&T	wrap & turn (see
CO	cast on	M1R	make one right-lean-	Sk	skip		specific instructions
cont	continue		ing stitch	Sk2p	sl 1, k2tog, pass		in pattern)
dec	decrease(es)	MC	main color		slipped stitch over	WE	work even
DPN(s)	double pointed	P	purl		k2tog: 2 sts dec	WS	wrong side
	needle(s)	P2tog	purl 2 sts together	SKP	sl, k, psso: 1 st dec	WYIB	with yarn in back
EOR	every other row	PM	place marker	SL	slip	WYIF	with yarn in front
inc	increase	PFB	purl into the front and	SM	slip marker	YO	yarn over
K	knit		back of stitch	SSK	sl, sl, k these 2 sts tog		
K2tog	knit two sts together	PSSO	pass slipped stitch	SSP	sl, sl, p these 2 sts tog		
KFB	knit into the front and		over		tbl		
	back of stitch	PU	pick up	SSSK	sl, sl, sl, k these 3 sts		
K-wise	knitwise	P-wise	purlwise		tog		
LH	left hand	rep	repeat	St st	stockinette stitch		
		Rev St st	reverse stockinette	sts	stitch(es)		

Knit Picks yarn is both luxe and affordable—a seeming contradiction trounced! But it's not just about the pretty colors; we also care deeply about fiber quality and fair labor practices, leaving you with a gorgeously reliable product you'll turn to time and time again.

THIS COLLECTION FEATURES

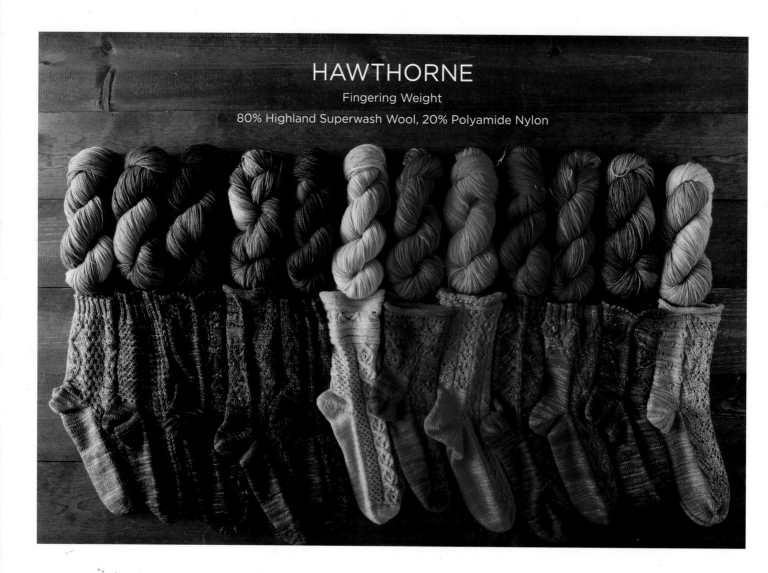

HAWTHORNE
Fingering Weight
80% Highland Superwash Wool, 20% Polyamide Nylon

View these beautiful yarns and
more at www.KnitPicks.com